ST AUGUSTINE
OF
CANTERBURY

ST AUGUSTINE
OF
CANTERBURY

MICHAEL A. GREEN

JANUS PUBLISHING COMPANY
London, England

First published in Great Britain 1997
by Janus Publishing Company
Edinburgh House, 19 Nassau Street
London W1N 7RE

British Library Cataloguing-in-Publication Data.
A catalogue record for this book is available from the British Library.

ISBN 1 85756 366 2

Cover design Harold King

Photoset by Keyboard Services, Luton
Printed and bound in England by
Antony Rowe Ltd,
Chippenham, Wilts

ST AUGUSTINE OF CANTERBURY

Celebrating 1,400 years of his arrival in England

MICHAEL A. GREEN

'. . . it was also to get the pagans to give glory to God for his mercy, as scripture says in one place; "For this I shall praise you among the Pagans and sing your name".'

St Paul to the Romans 15, Roman Missal

CONTENTS

ILLUSTRATIONS

Photographs of relevant sites in south-east Kent appear
between pages 18 and 22.

FOREWORD

The year 1997 marks celebrations commemorating the arrival in England of St Augustine and his monks to convert the pagan Anglo-Saxons. One thousand four hundred years have gone by since his arrival. None the less this momentous event still continues to influence Christians down to the present day. Naturally, the detailed records of what happened 1,400 years ago are very sparse. In the main they have to rely upon word of mouth and memories of those who at some later time wrote down the circumstances which they had seen had such significance for their own Christian Faith and for the future. Michael Green continues in this tradition of reflection and commenting upon the significance of the arrival of Augustine for the people of his time. In so doing, of course, he underlines to us our own inheritance and our own responsibility for the future of continuing to sustain and transmit the Christian Faith to those who come after us.

We are particularly fortunate in that some of the correspondence from those early days between Pope Gregory and Augustine is preserved in Bede's *Ecclesiastical History* and in Pope Gregory's *Register*. While some modern professional historians have doubted the full accuracy of the picture drawn by the Venerable Bede, none the less, the general outlines are certain. A monk came from Rome sent by Pope Gregory, with his companions, to convert the pagan Anglo-Saxons in the south-east corner of England. Their

Foreword

mission was eminently blessed and successful. It laid the foundations for Christianity in England which had been over-run by the invaders from the Continent after the Roman armies had withdrawn. Despite the passage of centuries the spirit of Christianity still flourishes in England. However, there is still much to do to remind our contemporaries of their inheritance so that they too may turn to Jesus Christ the Universal Saviour.

Bishop John Jukes O.F.M. Conv.,
Bishop of Strathearn,
Auxiliary Bishop in Southwark

ACKNOWLEDGEMENTS

I am indebted to Bishop John Jukes for his observations on the text of this book and for his writing the Foreword.

Many thanks to Dr Michael Stainton for supplying information on a trip the 'Friends of the Holy Father' took along the route that St Augustine and his forty monks took to Canterbury from Rome; also to Canon Michael Bunee for corroborative information on this venture.

Thanks are due to my wife Joanne, for her patience, to Fr John Slater for his encouragement, and to Angela Gillmore for transcription of longhand into readable word-processed perfection.

M.A.G.

PROLOGUE

'*Ite missa est*,' chanted the tall, olive-skinned priest; from the distinguished congregation came the response, '*Deo Gratias*.' Echoing throughout not only the already old church of St Martin, Canterbury, but soon to ring out throughout England.

In the front of the congregation stood a strong, tall, blond man of middle age, by his side stood a dark, beautiful Gallic woman; both were wearing crowns on their heads.

St Augustine was the priest – Pope Gregory's missionary to England; the King was Ethelbert, King of Kent, at his side was his wife, his Catholic Queen Bertha.

After Mass, Augustine said to his friend and fellow missionary, Lawrence, 'This mission to England has started well, we have just celebrated Mass at Christmas in the year of our Lord 597, and it is only a short while ago that we landed at Ebbsfleet. The welcome and success in this city of Canterbury augurs well for it to be the centre of our mission to bring England to the Faith.'

May we all say in 1997 with that first congregation:

Deo Gratias

1

IN THE BEGINNING

Invasion of Britain by the pagan Anglo-Saxons drove a wedge between the Celtic/Romano Christians and the developing Roman Catholic Church.

St Augustine was the missionary sent by Pope Gregory the Great to convert the Anglo-Saxons and restore contact with the Celtic Church.

The Celtic Church consisted of 'primitive Christians' who had come over to Britain via Greek and Lebanese traders in the first century AD. They had their faith from the desert fathers and settled in Cornwall, Wales and Western Scotland. This 'Celtic fringe' was joined later by Roman Christians from the rest of Britain swept westward by the Saxon invasion. This group of Christians sprang largely from Roman Legionnaires who had covertly brought Christianity to Britain, while overtly worshipping Mithrus 'the God of Warriors'.

Later, the Emperor Constantine found Christ and expressed his faith as a discipline for life. To be a Christian was to become a member of a society with a great many rules and regulations with penalties for failing to observe them; a bonding of men and women of various races and cultures in the name of Jesus Christ.

A detailed history of this time was and is difficult to prove. It is true, some books were written and subsequently destroyed by the pagan Saxons. What is most relied upon is stories, no doubt embellished in the process of word of mouth passed down the years. Even the Venerable Bede was dependent on this process, and his is the most accurate record of this period.

Myths and legends abounded. One of the most popular by volume, thus lending some authority to it, is the legend that Joseph of Arimathea came with Saints Philip, Lazarus, Martha and Mary to Marseilles. St Joseph and the Holy women continued to Britain. 'They landed in the south-west coast and made their way to Avalon [now Glastonbury] bearing with them the Holy Grail [i.e. the chalice wherein our Lord consecrated the wine and water at the institution of the Eucharist and in which was said to be some of the blood which fell from the Saviour's wounds as he hung on the Cross]. On their arrival they proceeded to the people and, for a testimony, was pointed to St Joseph's staff which blossomed and became a tree immediately after he had planted it. King Arviragus gave them land and allowed them to settle.'[1] The mystique of this legend still prevails.

If all information was myth, legend or reported history by word of mouth, then such stories would not have been sustained. But by AD 565 a strong Saxon King (Ethelbert) sat on the throne of the Kingdom of Kent, and many think this was a very stable period in an era of instability. Ethelbert's capital was Canterbury, and to this city came Augustine, missionary of Pope Gregory the Great, in AD 597.

A detailed, chronological list of developments in the Celtic Church and among Roman–British Christians follows.

CHRONOLOGICAL DEVELOPMENTS OF THE CELTIC CHURCH UNTIL AD 597*

NAME	FEAST DAY	PERIOD	ACTIVITY
ASAPH	11 May	Sixth Cent.	Founder of Church at Llanasa, Flintshire
AUSTOL	28 June	Sixth Cent.	Accompanied St Méen (or Mewan)
COLUMBA	9 June	521–597	Abbot and Missionary With 12 companions settled in Iona, preached among the Picts
DAVID	1 March	Sixth Cent.	Abbot, Bishop. Patron Saint of Wales. Went on pilgrimage to Jerusalem and was there consecrated Bishop
DUBRICIUS	14 Nov	Sixth Cent.	Church leader in S.E. Wales and Western Herefordshire
GILDAS	29 Jan	500–570	Called 'the wise', said to be the author of *Concerning the ruin and conquest of the Romans and five contemporary kings*
GWINEAR	23 March	Sixth Cent.	Martyr-leader of a band of Irish missionaries who landed in Cornwall and were martyred by the heathen ruler Teudor
KENTIGERN or MUNGO	14 Jan	c 612	Bishop, native of Lothian, missionary in Cumbria. Founded the Monastery at Llanelwy
MÉEN	21 June	Sixth Cent.	Abbot. Founded monastery in Paimpont which was later named after him. Godfather to Austol
PATRICK	17 March	385–461	A Romano–Briton born near the Clyde. His father was a civil official and deacon, and his grandfather was a priest. Patrick was kidnapped by raiders and enslaved in Ireland. From background and experience he became very devoted to the faith and saw the need for conversion of Ireland. He returned from Auxerre where he had been ordained as a priest, to Ireland as a missionary Bishop. Patron Saint of Ireland

* Information gathered from *Dictionary of Saints*, Donald Attwater, Penguin

St Augustine of Canterbury

CHRONOLOGICAL DEVELOPMENTS OF THE ROMAN–BRITISH CHRISTIANS TO AD 597*

AD 101   Pope Clement died.

AD 101–167   Covertly, Roman Legionnaires in Britain practised Christianity spreading the faith to the British in and around Roman settlements.

AD 167   Lucias, King of Britain sent letters, praying that he might be made a Christian, to Eleutherius, Bishop of Rome (*Anglo-Saxon Chronicle* p.307).

AD 286   Persecution of the Church by Maximian Herculius. Churches burnt down and Christianity outlawed.

AD 301   St Alban, Proto-Martyr of England. Gave witness to Christ for which he was tortured and executed.

AD c304   Aaron and Julius, Christian citizens of Chester, martyred at Caerlon in Monmouthshire.

AD 313   Constantine, first Christian Emperor of the Roman Empire persuaded Licinius to agree to a joint edict 'To grant to all Christians equal liberty with older religions and to live accordingly'.

AD 314   Council of Arles. British Bishops from London, York and either Colchester or Lincoln attend (*The Early Church*, Henry Chadwick p.63).

AD c394   Pelagins preached that there was no need of God's grace for the attainment of Salvation; denying also original sin.

AD 429–30   Germanus, Bishop of Auxerre, came to stamp out the schism of Pelagianism. He also defeated the Picts and Scots at what is called the 'Hallelujah' Battle. By deploying a small force at strategic points he had surrounded a large host of Picts and Scots, by getting his small army to shout 'Hallelujah' from hill tops the Picts and Scots, thinking they were surrounded by a large army, fled.

AD 449   Hengist and Horsa invaded Kent bringing the Saxons to the shores of Britain.

AD 449–564   Angles, Saxons and Jutes drove the Britons to the borders of Wales and to the North.

AD 565   Ethelbert succeeded to the throne of the Kingdom of Kent. Extending its boundaries to the Humber. Saxons to the North became known as North Humbrians. Ethelbert married Bertha, the Catholic Princess of Paris.

* All information (except that with special reference) has been obtained from the Venerable Bede's *Ecclesiastical History of England*.

2

THE PLACE – CANTERBURY

Canterbury has played a substantial role in this country's history. From the earliest of time Canterbury has been an exchange centre of goods, cultures and faiths, as a result it had a great civilising effect on Kent as a whole. For it was no less a person than Julius Caesar who said in his *Commentaries* that, 'By far the most civilised inhabitants are those living in Kent'.[2] Of the rest of Britain he said, 'All Britons dyed their bodies with woad, wore long hair, with hair on their upper lips, but not elsewhere, and shared wives between a group of ten or twelve men.'

Such a picture probably existed several centuries later except that the primitive Britons of the Dark Ages were later invaded by the pagan Saxons, driving back both primitive Britons and their only civilising element, the Romano-Christians and Celtic Church, to the far north and west.

In these Dark Ages, Canterbury was a flickering light of comparative civilisation. Its location, a crossway of river and road, and the consequential activity helped to achieve its pre-eminence.

It was indeed a major city, in *British Cities – Canterbury* William Townsend describes the primitive scenario, 'Both upstream and downstream, about a mile on either hand, had hills approaching each other from the sides of the valley, turning the site into a shallow saucer rather than a trough. Into this hollow was a ford and the end of tidal water of the river Stour. To it came roads, even before the

St Augustine of Canterbury

Romans built converging systems of roads from Lympne, Dover, Reculver and Whitstable.'

A centre of excellence was thus established by the Romans on a place 'programmed' from early time. These contours that were so useful to the Romans were 'ways' from the west over Salisbury Plain, the Surrey hills and the North Downs. It was probably the way tin mined in Cornwall was carried to France, using Canterbury as a base for transshipment to both France (or Gaul) and Belgia (there was a Balgia settlement in Canterbury).

Thus so, man's three principles of maintaining life were ensconced in Canterbury before, that is, the advent of both Roman occupation and growth of Christianity.

Trade, to maintain a way of survival, military power to protect trade routes from marauders, and because man is imperfect and mortal, he had to aim for perfection and try to claim immortality through spiritual means.

Thus we see, in time the Druids walking the 'way' from the west, we see Pagan Britons worshipping their gods as did the Saxons and Vikings later. But Christ came first to Canterbury through the Romano-Christians, who, it is thought, founded two churches, one where St Martin's still stands, probably a chapel for Romano-Christians to be buried outside the walls of the citadel. It is also thought that the second to be on the site of the present cathedral. Thus linking Canterbury with Rome through Roman Legionnaires and merchants who in a century were aware of St Peter and St Paul.

St Martin's is considered to be one of the oldest in Europe in which Christian worship has been offered without break. 'Roman brickwork suggests that at one time a Roman Temple stood on the site – as quoted on the three panelled boards outside the Church.'[3]

It is at this church that the Catholic Queen Bertha, wife of Ethelbert, King of Kent, came to hear Mass daily with her Confessor, Bishop Liudhard, and upholding her Christian faith in the midst of a heathen people.

It was in this church that St Augustine said his first Mass

of Christmas, and it was at this church that later St Augustine baptised the 'most powerful King' Ethelbert and received him into the Church.

St Augustine had started his mission, but what of the man, who sent him? Where did he come from? How did he get here? It all started with St Gregory the Great, recently elected Pope in Rome.

3

THE MAN – 'NON ANGLI, SED ANGELI'

Six years before Gregory the Great became Pope in 590 AD, the story goes that whilst walking in a Roman slave market, he observed some fair-haired youths for sale, asking where they came from, he was told that they were 'Angles from Angleland'. His response to this is alleged to have been, 'It is well, for they have faces of angels and such should be the co-heirs of the angels of Heaven.'

Gregory, not yet Pope, was engaged in other responsibilities in Rome, but no doubt found time to research this place called Angleland. Firstly he no doubt read the work of St Gilda, c AD 500, called *Concerning the ruin and conquest of Britain* under the Romans and five contemporary kings, which gave a historical background to this 'Angleland'. He probably was kept informed about more recent developments such as the fact that Kent had stable management under the rule of Ethelbert, who was married to the Catholic Princess of Paris, and that she had taken a bishop with her to Canterbury. Such intelligence helped him decide that a mission was to be made to England. He would have led it himself but he was first occupied in a legation to Constantinople, then in charge of his monastery at Rome.

Gregory was consumed with the desire to send or have sent a mission to convert the heathen inhabitants, but when he became Pope in AD 590, he obviously could not go himself. It was customary to send an abbot on such missions. Pope

St Augustine of Canterbury

Gregory turned to his own monastery on the Coeliun Hill in Rome, where he had been the abbot. But, it would seem the abbot was too old for such a journey, so Pope Gregory broke with tradition and called the young prior to service, whose name was Augustine.

A Sicilian by birth, whose family background is not known, but on Confirmation he took the name of Augustine (after St Augustine of Hippo). He then entered a seminary in Sicily, where it is thought he became a pupil of Felix, Bishop of Messina. It may be the case that he received his education from Bishop Felix, who has been styled a *consodolis* (companion) of Augustine. Abbot Gregory was in any case very well aware of Augustine's ability and brought him to the monastery, St Andrew on the Coelian Hill in Rome, where Augustine progressed in faith and office, becoming sub-prior, then prior. Keeping watch over the lay stewards of the villas of endowment, that is, Church property.

He had by this time a considerable knowledge of Roman law. He also had the care of documents, with understanding and knowledge of them. He was confident in the relationship with the abbot; his brothers in Christ gave him their unstinted confidence.

Monks were not held together by fear of hunger or a changing society, but in co-operation, worked a life dedicated to God. To prevent any sort of self-destructive anarchy, be it material or spiritual, there had to be rules of operations. Such discipline was concomitant with faith, 'Because they dedicated their lives to God, in a peculiar way as the slaves of God (servi dai), they were trained in obedience and prayer.'[4]

Monasteries of this age were ritualised, but no elaborate ceremonial or singing was encouraged. However, Pope Gregory the Great introduced a common form of chant that became universal. It has a set form in a musical scale that most male voices could encompass in their recitation of the Mass and their Offices.

Augustine does not appear to be a charismatic leader of men, converting by cross and sword, but a quiet, devoted man who was a good organiser, an excellent administrator, but above all understood what type of mission Pope Gregory was now sending him on.

4

THE JOURNEY

So Augustine left his beloved Rome in 596 AD. Pope Gregory selected approximately 20 or 30 monks who knew their Roman law and Liturgy, but were also scribes, masons, architects and builders, to go with him.

As the countryside to the north of Rome was in a state of war, with the Lombards advancing on Rome, Augustine and his fellow missionaries went to the port of Rome and managed to get on one of the grain ships that traded between Rome and Marseilles.

On arrival they found that Gaul was also ravaged by civil war. Gaul had been divided between Clovis, the Conqueror's grandsons, which had led to constant fighting. This meant that travelling across Gaul was going to be slow, which in a way switched the plan of their mission for two reasons. Firstly, Pope Gregory had provided them with letters and documents to give to various bishops and abbots en route. Secondly, apart from seeing their Offices and admiring the scenery, it gave the group time to learn English, for it is possible they did not know the language of the country they were going to and communication would have been impossible and their mission very difficult without some knowledge of the language spoken in Kent. This was Saxon English, though through Queen Bertha there was probably a little Latin spoken in Canterbury, a language common in Gaul and Rome.

On leaving Marseilles, their first stop was at the Isle of

St Augustine of Canterbury

Lerins near Fraeus (where St Patrick had stopped for nine years). Augustine left the party at this point to make his first visit, bringing to Protasius, Bishop of Aix, messages from the Pope and fraternal greetings.

On returning to the Isle of Lerins, he found his party consumed with fear and dread. For they had heard from a 'reliable' source that the English cut the throats of those regarded as enemies, hung them upside-down so that the blood drained out and then drank it. They implored Augustine to go back to Rome to ask the Pope to rescind his mission. In sorrow Augustine did just this.

'The Pope in reply sent them a hortatory epistle persuading them to proceed in the work of the divine word and rely on the assistance of the Almighty.' This letter of order and encouragement contained the famous phrase, 'For as much as it had been better not to begin a good work, than to think of desisting from that which has begun, it behoves you, my beloved sons to fulfil the good work, which by the help of our Lord you have undertaken.'[5] Or, in modern parlance, with God's help finish what you have started.

Also in this letter, Pope Gregory said that on Augustine's return, he would be their abbot, saying, 'Humbly obey him in all things; knowing that whatsoever you will do by his direction, will in all respects, be available to your labour.'

With such an abbot and such a letter from their Pope, they moved on to Arles, a place of great beauty and peace, that by its buildings and environment reminded them of Rome.

Augustine had a letter asking Bishop Vergilius of Arles to give the missionaries advice and help for the next 700 miles of their journey. Vergilius was probably well informed as how the civil war progressed, the areas of conflict and those more peaceful. It is most likely that he advised going by boat on whatever river was in their intended direction, as this would probably have been faster than going overland and certainly safer.

While Augustine was discussing all these details with Vergilius, the monks were probably looking round Arles and wondering again how Roman influence had extended beyond Rome. Founded by Trophinus, a disciple of St Paul, in the first century AD it had the theatre and amphitheatre of Roman settlements of any size.

They continued their journey, on the advice of Vergilius, up the Rhone to Vienne, where they paused to give a letter to Bishop Desiderius, and from where they proceeded on foot to Lyons to deliver the customary letter from the Pope to Bishop Aetherius.

The journey was continued by boat to Châlons, where Augustine and the party met Queen Brunhild, who, it is said, gave them considerable help and advice, enough to warrant a letter of thanks from Pope Gregory the Great later.

Resuming the journey by road, bearing in mind that 'roads' were not as today, they were rough, but well marked routes through forest and by farm. It was a long, tiring haul before they reached Auton, a fortress town, heavily guarded. Bishop Syagrius was not only a friend of Queen Brunhild but also was in continual correspondence with Pope Gregory, from whom he received a letter from Augustine.

This town was very friendly, so much so that it became the 'natural break' to the Mission, and they stopped here for some time. Probably diverting visits were made to Metz and Orleans. Bishop Syagrius's help was so all-embracing that Pope Gregory sent him the *pallium* in appreciation (Bishops of Auton have the right to this distinction to this day).

Augustine and his party continued on their way, turning west along the River Loire, till they reached Tours. This city was the city of St Martin, famous as the founder of western monasticism. It was also the place where Gregory of Tours, famous historian of Gaul, had lived, to the previous year. Gregory of Tours had visited Rome in AD 594 and had told the Pope of the marriage of Bertha, a Princess of Paris, to King Ethelbert of Kent, and that she had taken Bishop Liudhard as a priest and confessor.

On leaving Tours they stopped at Port-de-Cé near Angers.

St Augustine of Canterbury

Here is recorded their first spot of trouble, and the birth of a legend.

Augustine and his missionaries had no sooner passed over the bridge in this village than they were confronted by angry villagers who hurled abuse at them and attacked them. God then intervened to protect the mission. Augustine raised his staff in protection and his arm stretched out like a bow and his staff shot like an arrow to a spot some 300 yards away. Walking fast to retrieve it he found that a fresh-water spring was gushing forth. Evidently it was possible that the village had run dry of water, and forty odd missionaries were going to deprive them of what was left. This apparent miracle solved the problem.

For next morning the people of Port-de-Cé found the missionaries had moved on to Angers. Partly in remorse, mostly in grateful thanks for this miraculous spring, they built a church on the spot, which is still there to this day – called of course – St Augustine of Canterbury.

Record of their journey from Angers is not clear. It is uncertain whether they went by sea, round the north coast to Boulogne, or whether they went by Roman road via Le Mans, Chartres and Paris. It is likely that they went by sea, as the turmoil of civil war would have slowed them down very considerably and by now they were good sailors.

On arrival in Boulogne they probably waited for a following wind to Kent, and spent the time in stocking up food, clothes and other supplies. It is also possible that by now they had a smattering of Saxon English. They recruited several Frankish interpreters to assist them on arrival.

One fine day they set sail for Ebbsfleet, then a thriving fisherman's port on the peninsula of the Isle of Thanet, stretching down to Stonar.*

Ethelbert, by now alerted to the arrival of Augustine, and his excited Queen, sent word bidding the mission to remain in Thanet where they were given shelter and food. The King called his 'cabinet' of thegns and advisers and it was decided

---

*A cross was erected in Ebbsfleet by Lord Granville in 1884.

to meet Augustine and his monks in Thanet, where the King insisted on sitting in the open air under a large oak tree, for fear of magic worked against him by these strange cowled visitors from far away Rome (this suspicion despite his Queen's chosen faith). But the monks advanced towards the royal party with Augustine in the lead and with his cross bearer by his side, the whole group chanting their hymn of praise in that medium that Pope Gregory had instituted.

Ethelbert saw they came in peace, not with fire and sword, and, with his Queen falling to her knees in front of the cross, he spoke to Augustine. If it were possible to hear their first greeting it was probably something like this, Ethelbert, 'I see you come in peace,' Augustine, 'May the peace of God be with you, noble King.'

Then Ethelbert invited them to his capital, Canterbury, and said they could commence their mission of conversion, subject to their not interfering with the running of the Kingdom of Kent.

It is possible that the party took to a boat again and went up the Wantsum Channel, past Fordwich along the Stour to Canterbury. Whereupon Augustine, on stepping on dry land, knelt with his party and sang the Litany, 'We pray thee, oh Lord, in all thy mercy, that Thy wrath and anger may be turned away from this City, and from Thy Holy house, because we have sinned, Hallelujah.'[6]

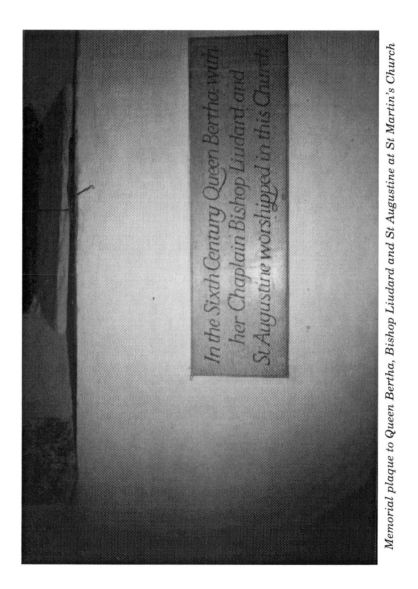

Memorial plaque to Queen Bertha, Bishop Liudard and St Augustine at St Martin's Church

Canterbury Cathedral viewed from the site of the grave of St Augustine

St Mary's Church, 30 feet east of the ruins of St Peter & St Paul Abbey later St Augustine's Abbey

*St Augustine's first grave in the Abbey of St Peter & St Paul
(St Augustine's Abbey) close by the front of the Nave*

The tomb of King Edbald of Kent (King Ethelbert's son) found in the porticus of St Martin

5

PROGRESS – AND THE NINE QUESTIONS

Augustine's landing at Ebbsfleet is thought to have been early in the year AD 597. It was a year that was to be the most active in developing the country until AD 1066.

With the aid of Queen Bertha, Bishop Liudhard and their band of Christian followers, Augustine and his missionaries settled in St Martin's Church as a temporary measure. Converts to Christianity started as a trickle, but soon became a roaring river as the Holy Spirit worked through Augustine and his missionaries.

On 2 June AD 597, King Ethelbert was baptised and became a Christian. By November, a chilly month in Canterbury at any time, some ten thousand converts sought baptism. For forty-odd monks, this was a large task. It could be imagined that they rolled their cassocks to their knees and waded out into the Wantsum Channel or the River Stour to perform this task, on a par with that other baptism by John the Baptist.

When Augustine informed the Pope of the event, Pope Gregory was delighted and probably led prayers for Augustine and the 10,000 English converts. What he did do was to send the *pallium* (vestment worn by the Pope or archbishops) to Arles where Augustine went to be 'ordained Archbishop of the English by Aethurius, Archbishop of that city'.[7]

Augustine returned to Canterbury, but Laurentius and

St Augustine of Canterbury

Peter the monk continued to Rome with a letter from Augustine. This letter to the Pope, and its subsequent replies, could be said to be the first letter in history that discusses moral and social questions of events in an ever-changing nature of society.

Augustine already had the authority of the Pope to reform, to adapt existing procedures and buildings, such as converting pagan temples into Christian churches. But it was to address the disciplines of a new Church from the archbishop's chair, and to assess the social problems that had been encountered, that the following 'Nine Questions' were asked of Pope Gregory.

It was some time before the Pope was able to reply. He was negotiating peace between the Lombards and the Eastern Empire, plus his ever-expanding role of Pope. As a result he began to suffer from ill-health and overwork. At one stage he was hardly able to rise from his sickbed to attend church feasts, and more importantly unable to preside at Mass.

But after a rest he was able to return to his tasks, one of which was to reply to Augustine, which he did in no uncertain way.

For exact details it is wise to read the original in the Venerable Bede's *Ecclesiastical History of England*, Chapter 27, but to give the reader some idea of the questions asked and answers given an abbreviated form follows.

Question 1: How do bishops behave to their clergy, and how are the things given by the faithful to the altar to be divided, and how is the bishop to act in the church?

Answer 1: St Paul's Epistle to Timothy outlines in Holy Writ that he should behave himself in the House of God. Clergy on receiving their stipends should keep under ecclesiastical rules, and live orderly lives, attending to the singing of the Psalms, and with the help of God, keep their heads, tongues and bodies from all that is unlawful. Emoluments which accrue are to be divided

24

into four portions, one for the bishop, one for the clergy, a third for the poor and a fourth for the repair of churches.

Question 2: Whereas the Faith is one and the same, why are there different customs in different Churches? And why is one custom of Masses observed in the Holy Roman church and another in the Gallican church?

Answer 2: Gregory reminds Augustine of the customs of the Church he was brought up in, but goes on to say, 'But it pleases me that if you have found anything, either in the Roman or the Gallican, or any other Church, which may be acceptable to almighty God, you carefully make choice of the same and sedulously teach the church of the English which is as yet new in the Faith, whatsoever you can gather from the several Churches. For things are not loved for the sake of places, but places for the sake of good things. Choose therefore from every church those things that are pious, religious and upright and when you have, as it were, made them up into one body, let the minds of the English be accustomed thereto' (Chapter 27, pp. 41–2). [This was, historically speaking, the Gallic Bishop Liudhard of Senlis, Queen Bertha's priest and confessor at St Martin's Church, Canterbury, but to the modern eye could be the very first statement by a Pope on ecumenicism!]

Question 3: How do I deal with theft from a church?

Answer 3: Judge the thief in a manner subject to his background, be he of substance or in want. Punish with charity in mind. A fine on a person of substance which would be severe enough for him to forgo the occasion of theft; stripes for the poor who are not able to pay a fine. Both are painful but if done in the spirit of charity and reason, should be a deterrent.

Question 4: Can two brothers marry two sisters, which are of a family far removed from them?

Answer 4: This may be lawfully done, for there is nothing in Holy Writ to contradict it.

Question 5: To what degree may the faithful marry with their kindred, and is it lawful for a man to marry his stepmother and relatives?

Answer 5: [The answer to this question was a long one and related to pagan customs of intermarriage, without there being an awareness then of genetic problems.] Divine law forbids a man to 'uncover the nakedness of his kindred, until at least the third or fourth generation'. To marry one's stepmother is a heinous crime, because it is written in the Law, 'Thou shall not uncover the nakedness of thy Father', as a son is the flesh of his father and thus he would be insulting his father by marrying his father's wife. The same applies to a sister-in-law because by marrying one brother, she is directly related to the other. Yet they are not on this account to be deprived of the communion of the body and blood of Christ, 'lest they be punished for those things which they did through ignorance before they received baptism'. Guilt on these actions are only wrong when the parties know it is wrong to do them, a sin of commission.

Question 6: Can a bishop be ordained without other bishops being present because of distance?

Answer 6: You are the only bishop of the English, but unless some bishops come over from Gaul, you can ordain bishops until such time there are sufficient bishops, three or four, who can be called together to ordain a brother bishop as witness to sacred ministry.

Question 7: How shall we deal with bishops of France and Britain?

Answer 7: We give you no authority over the bishops of France because the Bishop of Arles received the pall in ancient times from my predecessor, and we are not to deprive him of the authority he has received. But bishops in Britain are committed to your cure, the unlearned may be taught, the weak strengthened by persuasion and the perverse corrected by authority.

Question 8: Should a woman with child be baptised? How soon after the birth of a child may she come to church? How long after birth should an infant be baptised? How soon after birth can intercourse be resumed or a woman come to church while having a period? Such questions are asked because of the social practices of the English.

Answer 8: 'These questions are pertinent to you and I believe they are answered in the content of previous answers I have given.' [Such a wide-varying list of questions on social conduct must have taxed the Pope's patience, but he gave a detailed, long answer to them.]

1. No woman with child should be barred from baptism as fruitfulness of the house is no offence in the eyes of almighty God.
2. No prohibition should be made at a birth of a child, for a woman to receiving communion, as birth is not a sin.
3. Neither is there any prohibition in baptising a child at birth, especially in the case of imminent death of the mother or child.
4. Her husband should not approach her until the child has been weaned.
5. No woman should be forbidden to go to church whilst having her periods, nature is not a crime.

Question 9: Whether after an illusion such as happens in a dream, can any man receive the body of our Lord, or a priest celebrate the Divine Office?

Answer 9: Discretion is urged, as whether intent or accident the illusion in sleep is realised, if by accident, superfluity or infirmity of nature then communion can be given and Divine Office read after a washing of the hands. If by intent, of giving way to passions of the body, then sin should be recognised and absolution sought before the institution of communion or Divine Office.

Thus was the framework of Moral and Social Law set, adding to this the Dooms (or Laws) of King Ethelbert, which provided the basis of Common Law that has grown throughout English History.

6

ONE FOUNDATION – AND THE EASTER QUESTION

After Augustine's consecration as Archbishop of the English, he started to lay the foundation of the Church of the English.

As we have seen, Gregory the Great gave Augustine permission to use what was available. But he did not make London his base as that city was surrounded by hostile pagan people who were quite capable of destroying Christianity in England at its birth. So Augustine decided that Canterbury was the better place to make the centre of Christianity in England, with friendly people, over 10,000 converts and a King who had become a Christian, the 'seed fell on good soil'.

Augustine used St Martin's as his headquarters for the time being. Having observed an old idol house close by, he threw out the idols and converted it into a dedicated Christian Church, to be called St Pancras. Then he started to have built an abbey to house the ever-increasing number of monks, which was called St Peter and St Paul, later to be renamed St Augustine's Abbey.

But a short walk through the city wall stood another Roman Church not unlike St Martin's, but it was in ruins. Augustine had it restored and extended it in size and named it Christ Church, on which site now stands Canterbury Cathedral.

In AD 601, Pope Gregory dispatched a further group of

St Augustine of Canterbury

missionaries to Canterbury, to support Augustine in his work. These included Mellitus and Justus, who both played a very important part in the development of Christianity in the south-east in particular and England in general.

Among this party also were craftsmen of all kinds – masons, architects, scribes, etc. All were under obedience to their abbot (Augustine) and practised their faith based on the 'desert fathers', engaged in various works within the monastery. Apart from building and recording events they also trained further priests and deacons.

To expand the faith in administration as the knowledge of Christianity became wider, Augustine sent Mellitus to London (then the capital of Essex). Here then was dedicated a church to St Paul (our St Paul's is on the site of this church). Mellitus became the Bishop of London to whom King Sabert of Essex came and was converted to Christianity. In turn Justus was consecrated Bishop of Rochester, thus the Christian faith was spread throughout Kent, London and Essex.

Now it was time to deal with another problem in the wider picture of England. The 'Church beyond the pagans', the old Romano-Britons and Celts, cut off from developments in Kent and Rome by the invasion and consolidation of Saxon pagans, 'with the result that they were observing an antiquated method of calculating Easter'.[8]

This antiquated method probably existed in the way Christianity is alleged to have come to Britain, via the Celts who had contact with the ancient methods of calculating Easter, 'simply keep it at the same time as the Jewish passover, on the fourteenth day of the Jewish month of Nissam, whenever that might fall. When Easter was introduced at Rome (c AD 160) the feast as at Alexandria was celebrated on the Sunday following the Jewish Passover, which for practical purposes could be reckoned as the Sunday after the first full moon after the spring equinox.'[9]

Between AD 601 and AD 603 'Augustine, with the assistance of King Ethelbert, drew together to a conference the Bishops or Doctors of the next province of the Britons, at a

place, which to this day is called Augustine's Ac, that is
Augustine's oak on the borders of Wiccii and West Saxons,
and began by brotherly admonitions to persuade them, that
preserving Catholic unity with him, they should undertake
the common labour of preaching the Gospel to the Gentiles.
For they did not keep Easter Sunday at the proper time, but
from the fourteenth to the twentieth moon; which computa-
tion is contained in a revolution of eighty-four years. Besides
they did several other things which were against the unity
of the Church.'[10]

Augustine found the Celtic churches obstinate in the face
of pleadings, rebukes and historical fact stated by him. A
second miracle proved Augustine to be what he was, God's
missionary, and not some foreign prelate dictating formulae
of behaviour.

He drew a blind man from the Britons, whose clergy could
do nothing for him. 'Augustine compelled by necessity,
bowed his knees to the Father of our Lord Jesus Christ,
praying that the lost sight might be returned to the blind
man, and by the corporal enlightening of one man, the light
of spiritual grace might be kindled in the hearts of the
faithful. Immediately the blind man received sight, and
Augustine was by all declared the preacher of the Divine
Faith. The Britons then confessed that it was the true way
of righteousness which Augustine taught, but they could not
depart from their ancient customs without the consent and
leave of their people. They therefore desired that a second
Synod might be appointed, at which more of their number
would be present.'[11]

This second synod occurred at what is now called Banger
Island where seven British 'bishops' and many learned men
assembled.

By this time the 'feel good' factor had evaporated and
these Celtic churchmen regarded Augustine as stern and
haughty. They accused him of sitting in a chair awaiting
their arrival, rather than coming to greet them. But 'walk-
abouts' were not the practice of state or church leaders
in the south. Both kings and prelates, both subjects and

suppliants, were expected as a matter of protocol to bend the knee or kiss the ring in respect of those sitting on the king's or bishop's throne. This tradition thus became a barrier between the old and new Church.

'There were many reasons besides Augustine's possible failure in courtesy for a break between the Roman Mission and the British Churches. The obstacles to his success lay even deeper than the conservatism which had developed through generations of British isolation and the hatred of retreating before an advancing race ... The pupils of a great ascetic like St David could have had little sympathy with the humane Italian monasticism in which Augustine and his companions had been trained.'[12]

It was not until AD 673 under that great Archbishop, St Theodore, that the dating of Easter was observed in the Roman way.

7

THE END OF THE BEGINNING

St Augustine died on 26 May, thought to be in the year AD 604. A seven-year episcopate, which changed the English nation for all time.

'It could be said of this praepositus from the monastery and clivum Scauri, using the modern idiom that he "started something". He had brought to the English, Latin Christianity and Latin civilisation, he had brought them at very great risk, and he had worked very hard.'[13]

He replaced the Saxon worship of Wotun and Thor with the worship of Christ the saviour, who advocated Faith, Hope and Charity in place of Idolatrous Faith; Hope based on divine inspiration rather than strength of endurance; Charity (or love) instead of love only as a sexual pursuit. The brotherhood of man by the cross rather than the sword.

He brought about a system of written learning in Kent, he introduced systems of building construction and architecture. He brought the use of Latin liturgy, scriptures and the sacraments of redemption; in total, he brought a faith, a culture, and buildings that were to house this faith and culture that had a profound effect on the development of this country.

It could also be said that as a result of St Augustine's friendship with Pope Gregory and King Ethelbert, the ensuing conversations, suggestions and instructions between them and with St Augustine formulated a part of the character of the English, the ability to compromise, the ability to see the other man's point of view, the approval of pragmatism. If it works why change it, but if it doesn't work, changes must be made.

St Augustine's death was followed by the death of Pope Gregory the Great in AD 606 and that of King Ethelbert in AD 616. So in a short twelve years the 'triumvirate' of the advance of Christianity to England ended.

However, this advance did have setbacks. On the death of King Ethelbert, Eadbald, his son, succeeded to the throne of Kent. He was not at that time a Christian and practised paganism.

At the same time the Christian King of the East Saxons, Sabert, died, leaving his land to three sons who were all pagans.

Christians everywhere trembled at this development and Archbishop Lawrence, Augustine's friend and successor, at first felt that he and the Bishop of London, Mellitus, together with Justus, Bishop of Rochester, should flee to Gaul. These two bishops in fact did go to Gaul, but Lawrence hesitated and delayed his departure, out of respect no doubt for his dead friend Augustine and his mission to England.

'When Augustine slept in the church in the monastery dedicated to the blessed Apostles Peter and Paul, Lawrence still lingered, unwilling to follow Mellitus and Justus across the Channel. He had his bed laid in the church of the monastery and in the night he poured out prayers and tears for the state of the Church; and he slept and St Peter came and scourged him for thinking that he, a shepherd, could leave his flock in such danger, and the next morning he showed the stripes of the scourging to King Eadbald. The King marvelled that the Bishop should have suffered these things at the hands of the apostle, and at length he renounced the worship of idols and his unlawful marriage. He received the faith of Christ and when baptised he was careful to give his counsel and favour in all church matters as he could.'[14]

Mellitus and Justus returned to Kent, Mellitus becoming

Archbishop of Canterbury when St Lawrence died in AD 619. In body Mellitus was a sick man, but Pope Boniface IV urged him to allow his undoubted spirituality to shine through his bodily ailments. This was evidenced when Canterbury caught fire threatening to destroy everything before it, but another miracle of this period was performed by St Mellitus. Eaten up with arthritis he stood in front of the flaming city and prayed, the wind turned back on the charcoal embers of the city already burnt; Canterbury was saved by Mellitus's prayers.

Justus was the last of St Augustine's missionaries to succeed to the Archbishopric of Canterbury. His turn lasted but three years, as he died in AD 627.

Of the second group of missionaries that Pope Gregory sent over to help St Augustine in AD 601, only Honorius succeeded to the Archbishopric, on the death of Justus.

With this kind of help and the ever-increasing number of Kentish converts, who ranged from just ordinary folk seeking the blessings of the Trinity to those who went into monastic life to become priests and monks, the Church prospered with the help of the Holy Spirit.

Of the Church, it was soundly established, the See of Canterbury was left empty only for very short periods for the rest of the century. Archbishop Deusedit officiating from AD 655 to AD 664 and that great old man Theodore, who was Archbishop from AD 668 to AD 690 bringing consolidation to the administration of the See and commencing the English educational system.

Of the Christian House of Hengist, as well as the Kings Ethelbert, Eadbald and Earconbert, there were other members of this royal house who made great contributions to the growth of Christianity in Kent, starting with King Eadbald's sister Ethelburga, who married King Edwin of Northumberland. This king was slain by King Penda of Mercia in AD 633, and his Queen with the help of Bishop Paulinus fled back to Kent, where she established a convent at Lyminge and became its first Abbess.

Earconbert's wife Saxburga, on his death, ruled Kent for a

St Augustine of Canterbury

year then established an abbey in Sheppey. It was started in the year AD 669 and consecrated in AD 675. She was Abbess from the time she ceased to be the Queen until she retired to Ely to join her sister Etheldrede.

Earconbert's sister, Eanswythe, however, is reputed to have founded the first convent in England in AD 630 in Folkestone on the coast. In Folkestone's parish church, on 29 February 1980, a small lead casket was removed from behind a brass grille which covered a niche in the north wall of the sanctuary. Examination of the contents showed a single human skeleton, the relics of St Eanswythe.

So the link is completed from the cross erected in the last century on the site of St Augustine's arrival to the finding of St Earnswythe's relics in 1980 – a glorious part of Kent's history, a great demonstration of the Christian faith, but one not without adversity.

Augustine's mission and ministry was aptly summed up by the Venerable Bede, referring to the Saint's resting place in the Abbey of St Peter and Paul (St Augustine's Abbey), he relates that on the tomb is written:

Here lies the Lord Augustine, First Archbishop of Canterbury, who formerly sent hither by the blessed Gregory, Bishop of the city of Rome, and by God's assistance, supported with miracles, reduced King Ethelbert and his Nation from the worship of idols to the faith of Christ and having ended the days of his office in peace, died on the 26th day of May in the reign of the same King.

Deo Gratias.

Michael A. Green
26 May 1996
Feast of St Augustine of Canterbury

APPENDIX 1

Benedict's Law and Influence

In the spirit of St Benedict, there is ample evidence that Pope Gregory and St Augustine of Canterbury followed his rule in the tradition of the times:

> Some Abbots ruled their monasteries by this tradition consulting at will such written rules were accessible to them. For all monasteries the tradition that service to God in the manner of Christ's withdrawal to the wilderness was regarded as central, but to such service an urgent need to exercise Christian compassion might add the succouring of travellers or the sick, in the cast orphans or pilgrims.
>
> The copying of manuscripts was needed for the welfare of the monastery itself, the child oblates must be taught their letters, as well as Monks should be, unless they were of advanced age, psalters must be written and books of the scriptures for the lessons of the night office and for study, altar books of the gospels and commentaries and treatises on theology by the Catholic Fathers. The life of a monk was in no way pastoral; but if pagans surrounded the monastery and came for instruction, it was as much an alms to teach them the faith as to feed their bodies with bread.

Augustine of Canterbury, Margaret Deansley, p.135.

APPENDIX 2

Chronological Summary of the Mission of St Augustine and its development through the following decades

AD 596	Pope Gregory the Great selects Augustine; the *praepositus* of the *ad clivium Scauri* dedicated to St Andrew; to lead a mission to England.
AD 597	Journey across France (Gaul). Augustine becomes Abbot on returning from Rome in response to Pope Gregory's dictum, 'What you have started you should finish.'
AD 597	Augustine arrives in Ebbsfleet. Greeted by King Ethelbert and Queen Bertha. Mission develops at a pace. Ten thousand converts baptised.
AD 601– AD 604	Pope Gregory sends the *pallium* to Augustine, creating him the Archbishop of the English. Also sent are implements for building, church furniture and books for scripture. Augustine asks his Nine Questions of the Pope and in due course receives the answers, laying the basis for conduct in the English Church, with social problems answered. Easter question raised and deferred.

AD 604– AD 619	Augustine nominated Lawrence to succeed him and sent Mellitus to London as Bishop of London and Essex. St Paul's was built in London. Justus was raised to Bishop at Rochester. Cathedral built in Rochester. On 26 May AD 605 Augustine died. Lawrence succeeded him as Archbishop of Canterbury. Pope Gregory the Great dies in AD 606 and King Ethelbert dies in AD 616. Eadbald succeeds Ethelbert as King and reverts to paganism, as do King Sabert's sons in Essex, after his death. Lawrence remains in Canterbury whilst Mellitus and Justus go to Gaul. Lawrence has vision of St Peter urging him 'to stay and look after his flock'. Lawrence dies in AD 619.
AD 619– AD 624	Mellitus succeeds to the Archbishopric after the death of Lawrence (who has been described as a friend of Augustine and of keeping the Church going during a very hostile period.
AD 627– AD 633	Justus follows in the Archbishopric for three years and is followed by Honorius, a later missionary, in AD 627.
AD 634– AD 690	Building of places of worship was continued to absorb the ever mounting number of baptised Christians. A monastery at Lyminge, Minsters at Sheppey and Thanet, a church at Reculver. Archbishops of this period, Honorius and Theodore, built on the foundations of Augustine's *Opus Dei*. Christianity was established in England.

NOTES

Chapter 1 1. Rev. C. Lane, *Illustrated Notes on English Church History*, volume 1, chapter 1, p. 6.

Chapter 2 2. A. Handford, (trans.) *Caesar, the Conquest of Gaul*, p. 136.

3. John Boyle, *Portrait of Canterbury*, p. 38.

Chapter 3 4. Margaret Deansley, *Augustine of Canterbury*, p. 5.

Chapter 4 5. Venerable Bede, *Ecclesiastical History of England*, chapter 23, p. 35.

6. Ibid., chapter 25, p. 38.

Chapter 5 7. Ibid., chapter 27, p. 40.

Chapter 6 8. Dorothy Whitelock, *Beginning of English Society*, chapter 8, p. 155.

9. Henry Chadwick, *The Early Church*, chapter 5, p. 84.

10. Venerable Bede, *Ecclesiastical History of England*, Book 2, chapter 2, p. 68.

11. Ibid., p. 69.

12. C M. Stenton, *Anglo-Saxon England*, chapter 4, p. 110.

Chapter 7 13. Margaret Deansley, *Augustine of Canterbury*, chapter 6, p. 89.

14. Ibid., p.109.

BIBLIOGRAPHY

ATTWATER, Donald, *Dictionary of Saints*, Penguin, 1983.

BEDE, THE VENERABLE, *Ecclesiastical History of England*, J. A. Giles D.C.C., Henry G. Bohn, Yorks, Covent Garden, London, 1847.

BEDE, THE VENERABLE, *Anglo-Saxon Chronicle*, J. A. Giles D.C.C., Henry G. Bohn, Yorks, Covent Garden, London, 1847.

BOYLE, John, *Portrait of Canterbury*, Robert Hale.

CARPENTER, Edward, Cantuar, *The Archbishops in their Office*, Cassell, 1971.

CHADWICK, Henry, *The Early Church*, Penguin, 1967.

DEANSLEY, Margaret, *Augustine of Canterbury*, Nelson, 1964.

HANDFORD, S. A., Translation of *Caesar, the Conquest of Gaul*, Penguin Classics, 1951.

HILLIER, Caroline, *The Bulwark Shore*, Granada, 1980.

HOWARD, Sir Henry, *Augustine, The Missionary*, John Murray.

LANE, Rev. C. Arthur, *Illustrated Notes on English Church History*, vol. 1, S.P.C.K., 1894.

MIRAMS, Michael David, *Ethelbert's Kingdom*, North Kent Books, 1980.

RICHARDS, Jeffrey, *Consul of God, Life and Times of Gregory the Great*, Routledge and Kegan Paul, 1980.

STANTON, Richard, *Menology of England and Wales*, Burns Oates, 1887.

STENTON, F. M., *Anglo-Saxon England*, Oxford, Clarendon Press, 1967.

TAIT, James, *Medieval English Borough*, Manchester University Press, 1936.

St Augustine of Canterbury

TOWNSEND, W. and BATSFORD, B. T., *British Cities – Canterbury*.

WHITELOCK, Dorothy, *Beginnings of English Society*, Pelican History of England, 1952.